1 MONTH OF
FREE
READING

at

www.ForgottenBooks.com

By purchasing this book you are eligible for one month membership to ForgottenBooks.com, giving you unlimited access to our entire collection of over 1,000,000 titles via our web site and mobile apps.

To claim your free month visit:

www.forgottenbooks.com/free206894

ISBN 978-0-484-38463-6
PIBN 10206894

THE

INCARNATION,

AND

MISCELLANEOUS POEMS:

ALSO,

INFIDELITY,

A TALE OF THE REVOLUTION,

BY J. B. THOMAS.

COVINGTON, KY.

R. C. LANGDON, PRINTER.

1844.

PREFACE.

THIS little volume is not the production of one whose fate it has been to woo the Muses in Academic groves: its author, therefore, does not dare to expect that it should pass the ordeal of modern criticism entirely unscathed; or that it should appear at the bar of popular taste altogether uncondemned. His harp has, he trusts, been tuned to Nature, to Virtue, and to Truth; and he humbly hopes that these, his efforts, the interlines of ordinary life, may not only tend to amuse the mind of the reader, but lead to the contemplation of Nature, and of Nature's God; and aid in inculcating those moral principles which he has attempted to illustrate.

THE AUTHOR.

Covington, Ky.

THE INCARNATION.

IMMORTAL THEME! thy mighty matchless song
Through vast eternity shall roll along,
As waked by angel-hands from harps above,
It pours the music of Eternal Love;
While the loud anthem sweeps its ample round,
And all Heaven's echoes tell the rapturous sound.
Fain would I list your lays, ye spirits bright!
Invoke your aid, ye ministers of light!
And imitate your strains and joys above,
And sing the triumphs of *Redeeming* Love,
Sing of Salvation's work and wond'rous plan,
Where Grace and Justice met, and rescued Man.

Let thought retrace th' billowy stream of time,
Behold a Deity enthroned sublime,
Ere from the dark, the dense, chaotic deep,
He bade unnumbered orbs to being leap;
Ere from the chambers of eternal night,
At his command arose the lovely light:
Or from his hand Omnipotent was hurl'd
Upon its path this swift revolving world:
Ere it was clothed with grass, and herb, and tree,
Adorned and decorated, man for thee.

All this was done—and God pronounced it good;
Then roll'd the river, and spread forth the flood;
With foliage waved the wood-crown'd mountain tops;
With beauty bloom'd the valley and the copse,
While fruits ambrosial leant from every limb,
And bright-wing'd songsters warbled praise to Him;
Then laugh'd the rivulet as it leapt along,
Murmuring its music in perpetual song;
Then fountains gushed, and mighty oceans roll'd,
Broad'ning and blushing 'neath Heaven's beams of
          gold;
As daily walk'd the sun in majesty and might,
Or the mild moon led forth the hosts of night.

Then were the counsels of th' Eternal set:—
For 'midst these wond'rous works, no man was yet:
There was no voice to represent the whole;
Amidst this world of matter, was no soul;
No hand to tend the rich, luxuriant root,
To till the ground, or cull the rosy fruit;
Nor waited long this world, thus furnished fair,
Thus richly wrought with varying beauty, ere
Man, young Time's illustrious stranger, trod
The virgin earth, the image of his God:
Fit for full intercourse with angel high,
With God himself, with Heaven, and earth, and sky;
Fit for to rule o'er being's lower grade,
And to present them as their federal head;
Fit to reflect the moral light divine,
Of Him who bade him live, and love, and shine.

Whence came the blight that blasted Eden first?

And with its witherings the creation curst?
Changed man—for peace and joy, gave wo and strife,
And nipt the buddings of immortal life?
Man sinn'd; and guilty in God's sight he stood,
And justice claim'd with keen bare sword his blood;
While swift diffusive as the rays of light,
Sin shed its broad its universal blight,
And like a mildew fell its fearful ban,
On earth, air, ocean, beast and man.

At the cool hour of even's softer light,
In Eden's garden walked the God of might;
And Adam heard his voice: that voice before
That nought to him but life and joy had bore,
Now fraught with terror, strikes his trembling heart,
Like the first clap that rends the clouds apart.
With downy wing the winds no longer fan
The quivering foliage, and the cheek of man:
But 'neath their rage the fretted forests bend,
The drifted clouds in sombrous shapes ascend,
'Till Heaven's broad arch, cerulean calm before,
Is mantled with the scowling tempest o'er;
While God walks forth upon his stormy path,
Strewing the missiles of vindictive wrath,
And with successive flash red lightnings fly,
And thunders roll, and rattle round the sky.

But scarce had man God's righteous mandate broke,
Ere mercy to his wounded spirit spoke;
She bade him raise his death-dejected eye,
And pierce by faith futurity:
"Behold the vision of the cross," she said,

"Thy seed shall bruise the treach'rous serpent's head."

But soon the seeds of sin were widely flung,
And in unnumber'd forms to being sprung;
Hateful where'er — injurious to man,
And detrimental to God's gracious plan;
What fearful fruit that baneful plant has bore!
What madd'ning passions have man's bosom tore!
How many sorrows, and how many fears,
How many rivers have been shed of tears.
What wo, what murder, misery and crime,
Have stained with grief and gore the page of Time:
What bloody wars, what sacrifice of faith,
What pain, disease, and wretchedness, and death.

These were the devil's works : these to destroy
Appear'd a Saviour to the patriarch's eye.
A Saviour! Oh! 'twas Mercy's priceless dower;
He comes to save from sin and Satan's power:
To bring back peace on earth, and joy and love,
And link lost man to life, and God above;
He comes to consummate the glorious plan,
Retouch, revive God's image upon man:
Light up his passage through the gloomy grave,
And land him safe beyond death's stormy wave;
There to regain his long-lost high estate,
And smile triumphant over Satan's hate:
There to enjoy redemption full, complete,
And bask forever at his Saviour's feet.

How sweet the ray! though streaming far and faint,
By which the patriarch could the promise paint;

·How gladd'ning was its light! as first it shot
Athwart the gloom, and cheer'd his wretched lot.
The strugg'ling beam broke slowly on his path,
Chasing the darkness, giving grace for wrath :
Slowly but sure, it showed the Sun would rise,
To bless the world, and gild man's moral skies.

So when the sun, the dazzling king of day,
Upon the orient flings his herald ray,
The glowing brightness tells his gradual rise,
Nor bursts at once his grandeur on our eyes;
So slowly man develops all his powers;
So steals the Spring upon the wintry hours;
So rolling rivers rise from little rills :
So nature acts, so God in nature wills;
The God of nature, is the God of grace,
Harmonious all, and equal are his ways.

Thus dim the dawn, and feeble was the ray,
That mark'd the twilight of the Gospel day;
With mercy fraught, on Adam first it rose,
With Time's still broad'ning track, it brighter grows :
And on the mind of faithful Abram shone,
While angels whisper'd of the coming Sun;
Each new accession, thus man's mind prepar'd
For larger light, which Israel's offspring shared;
While David's harp in sweetest raptures rung,
And on the lyre of prophecy was sung
By seers successive through the lapse of time,
In strains of lofty eloquence sublime,
The glorious dawn, the day-spring from on high,
That soon should burst upon man's wond'ring eye.

" By sin came death"—and doom'd to death man
    stood;
The price of pardon, was the price of blood;
'Gainst goodness infinite did he rebel;
No finite being's blood could save from hell.
Nought but the precious blood of God's own Son,
Could for the sin-curst creature man atone;
Not all the rites and ceremonies taught
To man by Moses, ere salvation brought;
Not all the blood of goats or bullocks slain,
That ere was poured upon the purple plain:
Not all the victims that ere yielded life,
Beneath the thirsty sacrificial knife:
Nor fragrant incense that for ages curl'd
From golden censors, ere could save a world.
Not all the washings of the ritual law,
From man's dark soul, one stain of sin could draw;
But worthless all, and valueless, and vain,
Save as the symbols of a Saviour slain;
Save as they pointed to that peerless blood,
That from the slaughter'd Lamb of Calvary flow'd:
Save as the types, that feebly figured forth
That great atonement's sacrificial worth;
And led by faith the feeble mind of man,
Through them their glorious antetype to scan.

As the wreck'd mariner with anxious eye,
Waits day's first glimmer on the eastern sky ;
So watched mankind with long expectant gaze,
The Sun of Righteousness, whose healing rays
Should put the mists of moral gloom to flight,
And fill the world with Heav'n's refulgent light.

When the Mosaic shadows all should fly,
Lost in the glory of the Gospel sky.

Now on the willows Judah's harp was hung,
That harp that long its heaven-taught strains had rung
In tones prophetic, solemn and sublime,
Along the fast unfolding flight of Time;
And Peace her balmy wings had spread o'er earth,
And all things waited the Messiah's birth;
While learned Rabbi, sage, and sapient seer,
Deep versed in Jewish lore, proclaimed him near;
Thus earth with wonder waited the event;
While from heaven's balcony bright angels bent
With deep amaze, they left their heavenly joys,
To search this mystery of mysteries.

The appointed hour was come: great Gabriel heard
His high commission from th' Eternal Word:
And on the pure transparent ether spread
His wings of light, and swift to earth he fled:
Swept with disdain the clouds that curtain'd Rome,
Pass'd kingly palace, spire, and sumptuous dome,
Nor paused his rapid and untiring flight,
'Till Nazareth he reach'd, as morning light
Upon the glitt'ring earth in beauty broke,
And thus to David's chosen daughter spoke:
"Hail! thou art highly favor'd, blest of Heaven,
Behold! the promise unto thee is given,
To thee the power of God most high shall come,
Fear not, thou shalt conceive, thy virgin womb
Shall bear a Son, and thou shalt call him thus,
Jesus, The Christ, Immanuel, God with us;

His glorious kingdom shall forever last,
While time remains, when time itself is past."
He said, and rising on the solar ray,
Pass'd the dense atmosphere of terrestrial day,
Pass'd suns and planets that revolving shone,
Still tending up tow'rd Heav'n's eternal throne;
While to his view its bright'ning prospect swell,
And on his ear its ceaseless music fell.
But ah! so lond the song, so vast the joy
That roll'd in rapture round the ranks on high,
E'en Heaven itself seem'd limited and small,
And Heaven's own music reached this earthly ball.

At midnight's peaceful hour when all was still,
And the calm moonlight lay on lake and hill,
When with bright gaze the glitt'ring stars of night,
Look'd down on earth through clouds of fleecy light,
And Bethlehem's shepherds by the babbling brook
For social converse had lain down the crook—
Behold! descending on a snow-white cloud,
With glory glowing as tow'rd earth it how'd,
An angel rode, arrayed in dazzling light,
The shepherds fell and trembled at the sight:
"Fear not!" thus Heaven with mildest mercy broke
Night's solemn stillness, and to mortals spoke;
"Fear not, glad tidings unto you I bring,
This day in Bethlehem's born a Saviour, King.
Unto all people shall go forth his fame,
And unborn nations worship at his name."
He ceased, and suddenly upon the air
The hosts of heaven with hymn and harp were there,
While songs celestial floated from afar,

Burst from each cloud, and vocal seemed each star;
Ne'er heard the list'ning night or ear of earth,
Music so sweet as told the Saviour's birth;
While deathless hands o'er gold-bright harps were
      flung,
And cherub there and glorious seraph sung,
" Glory to God, th' eternal God on high,
Peace on earth, good will to man and joy."

Trace with the eastern sage that signal light
That walks in brightness through the maze of night,
Amidst the stars, the glitt'ring stranger glows,
And pours its lustre o'er that babe's repose;
While there the wise men with devotion meet,
Their homage render at their Saviour's feet.

'Twas Winter;— cold and bitter blew the storm;
When shrined within an infant's feeble form
The Saviour came, and in a cattle stall
Appear'd on earth, the glorious Lord of all;
No princely hands a downy couch provide,
A manger rude the cradle's place supplied;
No costly gems were there, save night had shed
Her sparkling pearls around his sacred head,
And sweetly there the young Redeemer lay,
His warmest bed, his softest pillow, hay.

But from his wond'rous and mysterious birth,
Pursue his kind yet suffering path on earth,
To that strange hour when Christ the God-man died,
And on the Roman cross was crucified.
Scarce had the sun twelve summers roll'd around,

Ere in the temple was the Saviour found
In deep discussion with the learned sage,
And the famed doctors of that Jewish age,
(That temple which ere long his anger swept,
That temple over which the Saviour wept.)

Witness his baptism—when from above
Appear'd the Holy Spirit like a Dove,
While through the glory-clefted clouds God shone,
And said, " Thou art my well-beloved Son."

Led by the Spirit then, for prayer and thought,
Away from man, the wilderness he sought;
There Satan, too, his raven pinions bent,
On hellish spite and bold experiment;
In vain he then gave visionary birth
To all the passing pageantry of earth;
Vain were his wiles, and impotent his power,
The Saviour conquered in the trying hour;
While angels watch'd and waited on their God,
Satan, confounded, sought his dark abode.

But now among the multitude he stands,
Truth on his lips, and virtue in his hands—
Now on th' mountain brow, now on th' sandy shore,
To man he speaks, as man ne'er spoke before.
At his command the trembling devils fly,
And back with haste to hell's dread caverns hie;
He bids the spotted leprosy depart;
He heals the sick, and calms the troubled heart;
He calls, and the dark grave gives up its dead,
The slumberer rises from his dusty bed—

Stern Death is startled in his still domain,
And yields his prey to life and light again.
He speaks, and straight obedient to his will
The storm is hush'd, and the wild winds are still;
He calms the fury of the fretted wave,
And forth he walks omnipotent to save;
His voice unseals the ear, unties the tongue,
And bids it move in eloquence and song;
The lame now leap, the blind receive their sight,
And the dark eye-ball drinks the living light;
Heaven, earth, and hell, confess him God,
And nature bows submissive to his nod.

Upon Mount Olivet the daylight fades—
And Jesus seeks Gethsemane's deep shades.
Come tread with silent step the tragic ground,
And guided by that sadly solemn sound,
In plaintive accents hear the Saviour cry,
"If possible, O let this cup pass by;"
While bursting from each vein, and opening pore,
His brow with bloody sweat is crimson'd o'er.

But hark!
What sounds are those amidst the foliage dark;
From whence those gleams that throw their fitful
      glare
Upon the thicket, and the peaceful air?
What means that babbling multitude, whose feet
Pollute devotion's holiest retreat?
They come! they come! the Roman banners wave
Above the flaming torch, the sword, and stave;
There Jewish priests, and scribes, and elders walk,

And foremost see dark-visaged Judas stalk;
Prompted by Hell, impell'd by lust of gold,
Disguis'd by friendship's ill-worn mask! behold
Him with an impious kiss his Lord betray,
While savage hands the Saviour drag away.

Arraigned he stands within the Judgment hall,—
The much wronged man, the mighty God of all;
No marks of coward guilt, or felon fear,
About that heavenly form or face appear,
No anger flashes from his eye serene,
Upon that placid brow no shame is seen,
No bitter, angry wrath, no murmuring word,
Upon those sweet and holy lips were heard,
But truth and love, without a single shade,
In purest lustre o'er his features play'd:
Behold his back the cruel soldiers bare,
The dripping scourge makes gory furrows there;
With guilty palms they smite his gentle cheek,
Insulting spit upon his face, so meek;
Deck him with gaudy, gorgeous attire,
And hail him King! in their sarcastic ire;
While the rude crown of twisted thorn is bound
His sacred and his bleeding brow around.
"Behold the man," the ruthless Roman said,
And Jesus forth for mockery was led;
In mimic majesty the Saviour trod,—
Man reviewed but man, where angels saw a God.

Then from the multitude assembled there,
Went up a shout that rent the ambient air:
"Crucify him! crucify him!" they cry,

" Release Barabbas, let this Jesus die."
In vain in his defence then Pilate stood,—
"On us and on our children be his blood."
And like the noise of many waters rose that cry;
It rose to God, 'twas registered on high.

Now the slow finger of Heaven's dial told,
That near some crisis in man's hist'ry roll'd :
Some scene to which the present and the past,
With deep'ning interest, was converging fast:
Some vast event, with mighty import fraught,
O'er which had ponder'd long angelic thought;
And while from Heaven, its ranks of glory bend,
Oft wond'ring where the mystic scene will end:
All Hell is roused, and Earth is rife with hate,
The great design of Heaven to consummate.
Up Calvary's rocky summit moving slow,
Methinks I see the strange procession go;
I see the Saviour bear that fatal tree
On which he died, and died, O man, for thee!
The iron enters now his quivering flesh,
At every cruel stroke it bleeds afresh,
'Till bath'd with reeking blood and mangled sore,
Aloft they raise the spectacle of gore.
Angels, look down, behold the awful sight!
Ye gazing devils, tremble with affright!
Ye mortals! listen to his dying groan,
Look, love, and live, and him your Saviour own.
Heaven stays th' eternal music of her lyres,
And nature shudders while her God expires;
The conscious sun with shame has veil'd his face ;
Earth 'neath its burden trembles to its base;

B.

The temple's vail, th' eternal rocks are rent;
Death opes his gates, and views the vast event;
For Jesus dies,—with plaintive voice he cried,
Then on his breast he drooped his head and died.

For him the new-made sepulchre prepare,
And gently lay the Lord of Glory there;
Bring precious ointment, aloes, spice and myrrh,
And linen clothes,—with tears your Lord inter:
'Tis done,—the painful, pleasing task is o'er,
And the huge stone is placed against the door;
The guards are set,—the silent sentry keep
Their patient watches o'er his transient sleep;
For on the third day, Jesus Christ had said
He would arise, and come forth from the dead.

'Twas midnight,—and no star the welkin wore;
Nature with darkness deep was mantled o'er,
And silence reign'd, except the measured tread
Of those who paced about the Holy dead,
And round that rock with cautious footstep crept,
In whose cold bosom the Redeemer slept.
'Twas vain to guard a God,—his hour was come,
An earthquake tells his triumph o'er the tomb;
An angel rolls the massy rock away,
And Death appall'd gives up his mighty prey;
The guards with terror struck as dead men fell,
While Jesus rose, Conqueror of Death and Hell.

As man, he died for man—but rose a God;
Again this sin-polluted earth he trod;
Around him gather'd his desponding band,

And cheer'd their hearts, and left them this com-
    mand:
" Go to all nations, and in every clime
This Gospel preach, until the end of time:
And lo! with you I'll be, my power and love
Shall guard on earth, and guide to heaven above."
Then round his form his snow-white robe he wrapp'd,
While hovering angels their glad pinions clapp'd,
As borne aloft beyond man's aching view,
The holy convoy pierced the azure blue;
Radiant with smiles, with glowing glory bright,
Their dear Redeemer left their wond'ring sight.
Meet him, ye hosts! who heaven's high places hold:
Archangels! tune afresh your harps of gold,
And with united anthem, loud and sweet,
Your coming God, our rising Saviour greet;
Let all the shining ranks of glory shout,
For man is saved, and Satan put to route;
Fling back the everlasting gates of light,
The King of Glory claims his native right.
The everlasting doors are open thrown,
And Christ sits down on his eternal Throne.

A God incarnate! Is the mystery o'er?
Eternity its wonders shall explore;
Its theme shall live on every angel's lip,
That from the fount of life eternal sip,
And ransom'd millions round the throne above,
Shall sing forever of Redeeming Love.
A God Incarnate! 'Twas the blessed ray
That shone at first on man's benighted way,
That lumed with glorious light along his path,

And broke the darkness of Mount Sinai's wrath;.
To Him the shadowy antetypes referr'd,
He was the substance of prophetic word,
The second Adam; the pattern pure of man,
When purged completely by the gospel plan.
A God Incarnate! Crucified for man!
Its vast results no mortal mind may scan;
Its blessed influence on the human soul,
Is boundless as eternity's long roll.
But not alone the soul's salvation 's wrought
By blood divine, but every blessing bought.
" By sin came death," and all beside,
Is mercy flowing from a Saviour's side:
That mercy ministers 'long the path of life,
Cheers and sustains amid the dying strife;
Pours its rich radiance round the dreaded tomb
That sin has reared, and tapestried with gloom;
Bears the freed spirit on its outspread wing,
To Heaven, forever mercy there to sing.

This great salvation, glorious, full and free,
With mighty power shall spread from sea to sea:
That purple spring 'midst Calvary's rocks that rose,
Whose wid'ning wave to every nation flows,
Shall, with the ransom'd on its bosom move
To the calm ocean of Eternal Love.
That Sun of Righteousness, whose crimson light
Chased the thick darkness of man's moral night,
Shall upward roll, until its bright'ning ray
Is merged amid the blaze of ceaseless day,
This blessed Gospel, fraught with truth and grace,
With joy and love, shall sin and sorrow chase,

'Till to all lands Truth's sacred stream shall flow,
And every heart its saving power shall know ;
'Till universal love on earth shall reign,
And sinful man his Paradise regain.

MISCELLANEOUS POEMS.

DEATH.

O DEATH! thou dreaded monarch of the tomb!
Whom nature robes with terror and with gloom;
Thou wilt ere long thy fatal visit pay,
And we must speed, with thee, from life away;
Must leave this old, this long familiar earth,
That, as a mother, we have loved from birth
No more to gaze upon yon glorious sky,
Whose wonders oft have woo'd the raptured eye;
No more to mark the ruddy morning rise,
Or day-light dying in the western skies;
Or evening hang her lamps of heavenly light,
In rich profusion o'er the glowing night:
All we must leave; each form we've loved to trace
From youth to age, on Nature's varying face.
Yes, at thy summons, we must bid farewell
To every verdant vale and flowery dell,
To every waving wood, and sun-lit hill,
To every ocean, river, lake, and rill;
To all the gladness of the joyous spring;
To all the charms the months of summer bring;
To all the treasures golden autumn throws;

To winter's grandeur—storms, and frosts, and snows;
All human intercourse forever quit,
And burst each tender tie that time hath knit;
Each band of friendship or affection here,
That the poor heart had learnt to love too dear.
Though long and dreamless then shall be our sleep,
Yon radiant sun his wanted course shall keep,
And sweetly smile around the unprized spot,
Where me may lie, uncherished and forgot;
There her pale gleam the gentle moon shall fling,
Or midnight darkness spread her raven wing;
And o'er our breasts Earth's future sons shall tread,
Nor stop to think of the unconscious dead.
But ne'er from that deep slumber shall we wake,
Until th' Archangel's voice creation shake;
Until, from pole to pole, from shore to shore,
Earth hears the startling cry, "Time is no more!"
Then, at the trumpet's tone, the dead shall rise,
To meet their God in grandeur in the skies.

THE SOUL.

What is life worth?   Go take the tempest's wing,
And fly where winds their wildest dirges sing
O'er the poor mariner, whose final clasp
The floating wreck's last remnant grasp;
And listen, while the billows o'er him break,
To his heart-rending cries, and dying shriek;

Or turn and seek the sinner's latest bed,
To which a life of wickedness has led.

What is knowledge ? A precious gem that lies
Hid beneath this world's fashionable guise:
See Archimedes on the sandy shore,
Solving his problem 'midst the battle's roar :
Behold immortal Newton scale the sky ;
He lived for knowledge, but to know must die.

Or what is glory ? Ask the warrior train,
Their laurels gathered on the gory plain :
Ask the bold voyager, who through strange seas,
For fame, have braved the battle and the breeze :
Or ask the poet, by the midnight flame
Wasting his health, to purchase him a name.

And wealth ! what art thou, men so dearly prize?
The rich, the poor, the ignorant, the wise ;
Grasp'd more tenacious by the miser gray,
Than by the wretch who dies of penury.

Pleasure ! For thee, how mankind task each thought;
Each power inventive 's into action brought :
For thee, life's gay and giddy rounds they run,
And chase the phantom to life's sinking sun.

But what is giddy pleasure ! sordid wealth !
Knowledge, or glory ? bought with ease or health ;
Or life itself? each, any, or the whole,
Thrown in the balance, weigh'd against the soul ?
Go to the altar — see the sinner there,

His heaving bosom and his eye of pray'r;
Mark the big tear-drops o'er his cheeks that roll,
And hear,— he cries, Have mercy on my soul.
For it the martyr at the stake will die,
Joy in his breast, and triumph in his eye.
But O! to Calvary's awful summit fly,
Behold! for souls, a God, a Saviour die.

HAPPINESS.

Man's primeval bliss by sin blasted, destroy'd,
He ne'er shall regain, until God be his guide,
Through th' dark paths of error still wand'ring shall
     go,
But happiness find not, ah never! oh no!

We seek it at first in the follies of Youth,
(Disdaining the lessons of wisdom and truth,)
In the morning of life, 'mid the young spirit's glow,
But we meet it not there, ah never! oh no!

We seek it in Friendship—while warm is the heart,
That fondly would deem nought such friendship
    could part.
Those friends are all fled, when the storms of life
    blow,
And 'tis not in Friendship, ah never! oh no!

We seek it in Nature,—we bow at her shrine,
And almost believe all her beauties divine;
When false proves the world, here for solace we go,
But 'tis not in Nature, ah never! oh no!

We seek it in Pleasure,—through life's sunny hours,
And unthinkingly grasp its gay gilded flowers,
Nor dream of the thorn, that implanted below,
Says it is not found here, ah never! oh no!

We seek it in Love—in its impulses sweet,
We fancy at length we the fugitive meet;—
Its griefs and its joys in one chequer'd stream flow,
And it is not in Love, ah never! oh no!

In Honor we seek it: but what's in a name?
Though brightly emblaz'd on earth's annals of fame,
Though down to the future immortal it go,
It can't Happiness give, ah never! oh no!

Some seek it in Wealth,—how absurd is the thought!
To fancy true bliss with earth's trash can be bought!
Its pomp, and its pride, and its glittering show,
Cannot happiness buy, ah never! oh no!

Where then shall we seek it, where then shall we find,
True joy for the heart, and true peace for the mind?
Let loose every trust that this world can bestow,
Or ne'er will you find it, ah never! oh no!

Go follow the Saviour up Calv'ry's rude steep,
'Neath th' blood-dripping cross in true penitence weep,

Whom nature owns God, you your Saviour must
    know,
Or never be happy, ah never! oh no!

Here's happiness perfect, though not in degree,
But fully complete shall that happiness be,
When th' soul shall arrive in that world where **no**
    wo,
Shall ere break its repose, ah never! oh no!

WHAT IS LIFE?

A BUBBLE, on the billowy main,
A dew-drop, on the twinkling plain,
A meteor, in the midnight gloom,
A shuttle, in the weaver's loom,
A stream, that to the ocean hastes,
A morning cloud, that quickly wastes,
A flower, that fades ere noontide bright,
A verdant mead, cut down ere night,
A breath, that heaves the beating heart,
A stage, and brief each actor's part,
A tale, that no remembrance makes,
A brittle thread, that easy breaks,
A vale of tears, where sorrows dwell,
A path, that leads to Heaven or Hell,
A race, its goal the silent grave,
A day, the soul to lose or save.

MOONLIGHT MUSINGS.

THE sun has gone down in the gold-curtained west,
All nature has sunk into calmness and rest,
Nought breaks the deep silence, from man, beast or
      bird,
Save th' far distant waterfall, nothing is heard.

Majestic in beauty, the queen of the night,
Comes forth from the east, with her cohorts of light,
Not a breath from th' breeze, or from zephyr a sigh,
While th' mantle of glory falls soft from on high.

How gentle the hour! and how sweet is the ray!
Not gaudy, and glaring, and dazz'ling like day;
Nor fierce is thy beam, nor oppressively bright,
But placid, and peaceful, and pensive thy light.

Through the leafy-roof'd forest thy pencil'd ray flows,
Beneath light and shadow all lovely repose,
'Mong the dark-crested tops it streams down from
      above,
The semblance of innocence, purity, love.

Man sleeps,—and soft peace has descended on earth,
Now hush'd is its strife, and its turmoil, and mirth; -
How soothing the scene! here the wo-stricken mind
In its balmy influence, a solace may find.

The conflicts of faith, of power, and of passion,
The revels of folly, the nonsense of fashion,

In this hour with Heaven's own serenity fraught,
How little they seem, how unworthy a thought!

'Neath Heaven's own temple my homage I'll pay,
My prayer shall go up on its unsullied ray,
In concert with yon bright worshippers there,
Where sin never enter'd, nor sorrow, nor care.

BEAUTY IN TEARS.

' Beauty in tears:'—yes, she did look
    Like summer's lovely flower;
The reckless winds had rudely shook,
    That bent beneath the shower.

Nor met me, then, those eyes of glee
    That I was wont to meet,
Nor was her voice as 't used to be,
    To me like music sweet.

Her eye-lash fringe, with sorrow fraught
    Hung o'er its orb below,
Her lips were fix'd, and pensive thought
    Sat on her serious brow.

She spoke of disappointment's sting,
    How death her heart had tore,

Of joys that quickly took their wing,
  Of hopes that were no more.

I told her of a changeless rest,
  One firmer than a brother,
'T was a balm to her bleeding breast,
  Nor needed she another.

LANGUAGE IS WEAK.

LANGUAGE is weak, when it would tell
  Those gushes of the generous soul,
That wake within the rapturous swell,
  Or bid the gentle tear-drop roll.

For there are feelings in the breast,
  That never yet have utterance found;
And thoughts that still in embryo rest,
  That never yet were breathed in sound.

Hid in the fountains of the soul,
  Like pearls in Ocean's depths that lie,
Though o'er them many a billow roll,
  Or many an angry tempest fly.

Still will those depths sometimes be stirr'd,
  Roused by an incident, or thought,
A look, a smile, perhaps a word,
  And into life a moment brought.

Oft have we wished the mental might,
  To grasp this jewelry of mind,
And to bring forth, to life and light,
  All in the spirit that's enshrined.

But ever vain, must prove in part,
  The power of language to portray
The mysteries of the human heart,
  Its loves, and hopes, and sympathy.

VIRTUE.

THIS world's a chequer'd scene, where flows
A mingling stream of joys and woes;
This life's a shadowy rugged path,
And few the gleams of good it hath;
Delusive rays of fancied bliss,
Oft tempt man's wayward feet amiss,
' Till from th' dangerous dizzy steep
He falters to the fearful deep.
But there are spots of purer light,
Where Virtue sheds its radiance bright,
Pouring its joyous beams, heaven-blest!
Around the worn-world-wearied breast,
And leading far the faith-fix'd eye,
To worlds of light and love on high.
Thy blessings these,—'tis Virtue's here
The lorn and lonely heart to cheer,

O'er earth to bid the spirit rise,
And grant a charter for the skies.
Oh! had we kept thine humble way,
Nor sought the mazy world to stray,
Had kept thy upward pathway still,
When starting by life's babbling rill,
And left afar the world's wild shout,
Nor from. thy sure calm course turu'd out,
Still heedless of the Syren's song,
Had urged thy bright'ning track along,
How had we 'scaped ten thousand snares,
And half life's load of woes and cares;
Been saved from many a fearful fall,
From many a grief and bitter thrall;
Then memory her review might make,
Nor from the past one spectre wake,
Of blighted hopes, or murder'd hours,
Of blessings spurned, or misused powers.
When trembling by the crumbling grave,
Nature obeys the summons gave,
The soul her half-averted eye
Would glance o'er life without a sigh:
Angelic Virtue waiting by,
To aid its pinions to the sky.

VIEW OF AN ANCIENT CASTLE BY MOONLIGHT.

How solemn stands yon venerable tower!
Yon crumbling pile slow mould'ring every hour:
Doom'd to destruction — all its pomp sublime
Mark'd by the ruthless hand of hoary Time.
There darkness lurks, and gloomy horrors reign,
And desolation holds her dim domain.
How sweet the moonlight trembles o'er the scene!
Gilds the gray front, and flings her pallid beam
'Mong awful shades, and from her chill retreat
Drives ebon night, and shows her dreary seat,
Streams through the rugged chinks where moping
      sits,
The moody owl, while now and then by fits
The flaunting ivy flutters in the gale.

PARTING.

O! THERE'S a noble glow of feeling,
   Barren words can never tell,
Told when the tear is silent stealing
   From its deep and crystal cell;
Told by the warm, the heartfelt grasp,
   When we bid the sad adieu,

Lingering, reluctant to unclasp,
   The hand that tells the heart is true;
Told by the soft, spontaneous sigh,
   Heaving from th' burden'd breast;
Told by the love-lit tell-tale eye
   Where affection is confest.

PAST, PRESENT, AND FUTURE.

MIDWAY in life's rough paths we pause,
   And on the past reflect,
Sigh o'er the blessings that are gone,
   And those we have, reject.

For Memory, the time-dimm'd past,
   With loveliness arrays;
While Hope, upon the future throws
   Her bright illusive rays.

Time has its record borne away—
   'Tis stereotyped on high;
Nor will the future lift its veil,·
   To man's inquiring eye.

The present moment, then, demands
   Our most assiduous care,
With which to weave life's warp, and for
   The future to prepare.

For there's a future, seen by faith,
   A realm of ceaseless rest,
Beyond the bounds of changeful Time,
   Where Virtue shall be blest.

THE SAPPHIRE GATHERER.

In Cambria's wilds, mid rocks and hills,
And lonely glens, and mountain rills,—
For many a rock, and mountain bare,
And many a shadowy glade are there —
A peasant lived, retired, remote,
Close by some cliffs of lofty note,
That far their dark'ling shadows threw,
Adown whose sides the sapphire grew;
Hard by, there was by nature left
A dreary chasm, rudely reft,
Traditions tragic tongue had gave
The well-known name of 'Rennel's Cave.'
These to his cottage sometimes brought
Th' enthusiast wanderer, who sought
Nature in her own native dress,
And woo'd her in her deep recess.
   Fortune had smiled upon his birth,
But soon forsook him, and now earth
A desert seemed, friendship was lost —
Friendship, that flies when wanted most;—
Still he was kind, his board though scant

Supplied the way-worn trav'ler's want;
Nature he mused on, and his grief
Found sympathy, but not relief.
Feelings by man repulsed, returned,
And cent'ring in his bosom burned,
Strongly, with a soul grappling life,
Towards his sweet babes, and lovely wife,
But haggard want, and drear distress,
And penury came 'fore his face;
He could not see his wife in tears,
That now she stays, but not her fears;
He could not hear his children cry,
'Oh, feed me, Father, or I die.'
  On the bold cliff whose jutting brow,
Frown'd o'er the fearful gulf below,
Oft in his rambles he had been,
And there the sapphire-gatherer seen,
Attach upon its dizzy tip,
The trusty rope, and downward slip,
Fearless; while from the hoary chinks
He culls the costly weed, nor thinks
Of coward danger in his bold emprise;
(So much in custom courage lies.)
  'Twas in November chill and bleak,
Distress appear'd his heart to break;
One meals' short pittance for the day,
So scant it could not nature stay,
Was all they had; this little fail'd,
Nor care nor industry avail'd;
The babe hung on the breast in vain,
Its mother could not life sustain;
The child that play'd around his knee,

With healthy and untainted glee,
Now wore a weak and sickly hue,
And seem'd to fade before his view;
Hungry they leave the cheerless hearth,
No more the scene of social mirth,
And on their wretched pallet seek
A shelter from the blast so bleak.
   At morning light the peasant rose,
Strong purpose in his bosom glows,
And to the beetling cliff he hies;
The dangerous task he boldly tries:
The bar is fix'd, the rope is flung,
Above the dread abyss now hung;
He down the dangling rope descends
Unto a ledge, that inward bends,
Where from each cleft and crevice peep
The hardy natives of the steep;
Eager the precious weed to clasp,
The cord forsakes his trembling grasp,
His busy search still he pursues,
Nor yet his situation views,
'Till laden well, with cheerful hope
He glad returns,—but ah! the rope
His reach at baffling distance mocks;
Above him rear the scaleless rocks,
Beneath him rolls the restless surge,
O'er broken points the billows urge,
So far below, the ships there float
Seemed dwindled to a fisher's boat;
To heaven he lifts his earnest eyes,
In bitter anguish burst his cries:
His list'ning ear no answer found,

Save hollow echo gossip'd round,
In vacant mockery the sound.
Despair now seems his soul to freeze,
Around no help, no hope he sees,
But thinks those rocks his dying bed,
Sees vultures hovering o'er his head,
And many a storm and winter past,
His bones still whit'ning in the blast.

But on the cliff's extremest verge,
His frantic wife and children urge:
Borne by the breeze, their piercing cries
Arouse his spirit's energies;
And banish'd hope his breast regains,
One hope, one effort, still remains:
He paused a moment — he was young,
Courageous, resolute, and strong—
Summon'd each power, each nerve he braced,
Resolved now life or death to taste:
Into the dreadful void he sprung,
Dash'd at the trembling cord, and clung.
Again he is restor'd to life,
Again he clasps his babes and wife;
'Tis vain such meeting here to paint,
Pencil's too coarse, colors too faint.

SAMARIA'S DAUGHTER.

'TIS NOON—the sky is clear and cloudless—
And from his high imperial throne, the Sun
Unceasing pours a flood of fervid light,
Upon the pensive and reposing earth;
The distant woods in breathless beauty bow,
The beasts have fled, and in the thicket deep,
Or forest dense, or cool o'er-arching glade,
Have sought a covert from the gaze of day.
All, man and beast, some shelt'ring shade have found,
And moody wait the balmier hours of eve:
All, all save one, behold along yon path,
Whose silvery brightness through the landscape
        gleams,
The Saviour walks, leading his faithful few:
Heedless of heat, he treads with patient step,
And weary fever'd foot, the burning dust,
Bent on that glorious work of heavenly grace,
For whose accomplishment he came to earth.
But now he gains yon mountain's welcome shade,
Deep from whose base the crystal waters spring,
And there upon a gray and jutting rock
In thought mysterious,—human and divine,—
Sat earth's illustrious Guest: nor sate he long,
Ere from the city near, that peer'd in view,
As was her wont, Samaria's daughter came,
The bright translucent beverage to draw,
From out the cold dark depths of that famed well,

Where Israel oft had cool'd his hoary lip,
And led at Summer's eve his herds to drink.
Adown its moss-grown sides, the bucket dropp'd,
And quick returned. ' Give me to drink,' said he:
To whom the wond'ring woman thus replied;
' Thou art a Jew, why askest thou of me ?'
' Didst thou know me,' he said, ' thou wouldst have
    ask'd,
And I to thee had living water gave.'
' From whence, sir, hast thou it ? art greater thou
Than Jacob, who to us this water gave ?'
' He who this water drinks shall thirst again,
But who drinks that which I to him will give,
Shall ne'er for earth's polluted waters pant,
But it shall be a fountain pure within,
Still springing up unto eternal life.'

ON THE DEATH OF A MOTHER.

My Mother ! O the music of that word—
Though strange, now on my tongue—is never heard,
But in my soul some tender chord is stirred,
That thrills responsive to affection's power.
A mother's love is sure earth's sweetest flower.
Ah! who can estimate a mother's love ?
'Tis kin to that which burns in breasts above,
Seeming as sinless as an angel's love;

'Tis deep, abiding, changeless, and sincere,
Beaming through smiles, or bursting in a tear.

To memory's retrospective eye
A vision rises of the days gone by;—
First waked by memory's magic wand I see
Youth's sunny hours of gladsomeness and glee;
But gathering o'er that bright and morning sky,
I see portentious shades of sorrow fly;
Distinctly mark'd upon the darkling storm,
All robed in light, I see a Mother's form,—
Those eyes still beaming with her dying love,
That face reflecting all the bliss above.

Ah! there was one, a playful, happy boy,
So full of hope, and innocence, and joy—
Existence sweet! he never dreamt life's sky
Would ere be darkened by a single cloud,
Or its fair flowers by wintry winds be bow'd;
And he a mother had who watch'd his glee,
And many a secret prayer and tear had she,
For this her only and her much-loved boy,
And as he slept, she'd weep for very joy;
But God that guardian angel call'd away
To live forever in Eternal day;
For wasting wan consumption came
With stealthy step, to desolate her frame;
Reckless like Time, but certain in its course,
Slow in its progress, fatal in its force.
But fear of Death ne'er dim'd her faith-lit eye,
His fleshless fingers she could clasp with joy,
Hail him as one commissioned from above,

To introduce her to a world of love;
For that Religion that through life sustained,
O'er feeble nature now supremely reigned :
She found it true,—and in her dying hour,
Gave proof triumphant of its power.
And those who in that privileged chamber met,
Shall ne'er the place, the sacred hour forget :
Shall ne'er forget the joy, the heavenly shout,
With which that spirit from its clay went out :
Shall ne'er forget the placid smile it left,
Imprinted on that form, by soul bereft;
Reflection sweet, of all the bliss above,
The Christian triumph'd 'mid the Mother's love.

TO THE MEMORY OF REV. ADAM CLARKE.

IMMORTAL CLARKE! thy strong capacious mind,
Was rich with all the knowledge of mankind;
Though vast thy memory, vigorous thy thought,
Still all was calm, to peaceful fervor wrought :
'T was Truth's great store-house, placid and serene,
Where no confusion ere was felt or seen;
And all its wealth was offer'd at the Cross;—
Compared with which he counted all things loss.
Wesley the ground-work laid in all its length
Of the fair fabric, to which Clarke gave strength,
Gave grace, and symmetry, proportion fair,
And shed a pure, and steady lustre there.

Brightly he shone—but with no meteor light,
Flaming and flashing o'er the brow of night:
But like the sun, emerging slow sublime,
He rose upon the shadowy arch of time:
'Till in meridian power we saw him shine,
Bright'ning and broad'ning, unto life's decline.

TO THE MEMORY OF REV. E. ROBERTS.

WEEP,—for that much-loved man of God
Lays low beneath the unconscious clod,
That form we proudly gazed upon,
To the dark mould'ring grave has gone.

Weep — for society was reft,
When earth the sainted Roberts left,
When his freed spirit spread its plume,
Beyond the reach of grief and gloom.

Weep — for with love and christian zeal,
He sought our best our highest weal:
Spent in Salvation's work his breath,
And clothed with conquest, fell in death.

Weep—for full well the church may mourn,
A pillar from its temple torn:
O sinner, weep! for weep you may,
Perhaps, with him went Salvation's day.

Weep — for no more that fluent tongue,
Shall pour in eloquence or song,
Its faithful and its heaven-taught strain
In Mortality's dull ear again.

No more he 'll raise the uplifted hand,
And point you to the heavenly land;
No more those faithful feet shall trace,
Their pathway to a Throne of Grace.

No more those lips shall move in pray'r,
No more that heart its burden bear;
No; earth's last pillow he hath prest,
And gone to his eternal rest.

Weep not, for now his sainted soul,
Soars far above the starry pole,
And palms of vict'ry he shall bear,
And live in bliss forever there.

SABBATH MORNING.

GOD of the morning! the bright sun
    Has rose at thy command,
And his majestic course begun,
    O'er the rejoicing land.

His genial ray begins to chase
   The wintry gloom away,
And gentle Spring awaits to grace
   Earth with her green array.

God of the Sabbath! let the Sun
   Of Righteousness arise,
Its race already is begun;
   The night already flies.

Brighter and brighter may it beam,
   With healing 'neath its wings,
Till every land has caught its gleam,
   Till every Island sings:

Until this wide terraqueous ball
   One mighty temple is,
Till all upon his name shall call,
   And one vast song arise.

TRUE ENJOYMENT.

O ask not a name on the annals of Fame,
   'Mong the proud and ambitious of earth;
O ask not for gold, nor the wreath of the bold,
   Nor the fleeting enjoyments of mirth:

For wealth may take flight, and fame 's a false light,
    That glitters but to lure and deceive;
And the wreath of the brave is pluck'd from the grave
    Where the widow and fatherless grieve.

O ask not gay leisure for fashion and pleasure,
    Those butterfly baubles of life;
Nor think for to hide in a mansion of pride,
    From the world's wo, sorrow, and strife.

But ask for a rest in your conscience-calmed breast;
    The bosom's bright sun-shine of love:
Ask a heav'n-written name, a registered claim
    To the unfading enjoyments above.

THE SEASONS.

See Summer's ardent heat intensely burn;
Next Nature's restless scale brown Autumn turn:
With lavish hand her blooming sweets display,
Ambrosial offspring of the solar ray;
Till Winter frowns, and with destructive breath
Blasts each fair form in universal death.
But lovely Spring comes gleaming through the skies,
Etherial beauty o'er the world shall rise—
Rise from the ruins of rude Winter's spoils,
    And bless the world with her propitious smiles.

SPRING.

HAIL! lovely Spring! thy genial ray,
Chases stern Winter's gloom away:
Nature from ruin rising sings,
And joy in human bosom springs,
For Winter's ruder reign is past,
The furious storm, the bitter blast,
And bird's are twittering in the brake,
And smiles are dimpling on the lake,
And falling showers, and sunny hours,
And bubbling rills, and opening flowers,
And insect hum, and bursting buds,
And murmur of the gushing floods,
Proclaim thee here, and bid man raise,
With nature, songs of joy and praise.

FAREWELL TO SUMMER.

YES, go, thou bright winged Summer, go!
  Along thy flowery track,
With all thy golden beauty go,
  I would not call thee back.

Round earth refulgent Summer, roll!
　Thou radiant one adieu!
Go, Queen of Nature, over all,
　Thy beauteous blessings strew.

Thou 'rt gone, — and tearful is the sky,
　The sear woods mourn thy flight,
The flowers seem resolved to die,
　Bowing 'neath sorrows' blight.

Though brief, yet bright, has been thy smile,
　Upon the changing earth,
Awaking o'er the teeming soil,
　Its beauty into birth.

Until with loveliness and life,
　Was clothed the verdant land,
And earth with perfect beauty rife,
　Waited the gatherer's hand.

Thus, when this varied life is o'er,
　And its last hours have come,
By Truth's eternal light mature,
　Should man be garner'd home.

AUTUMN.

THE buds and the blossoms of Spring are all dead,
The beauty and brightness of Summer has fled,
The cold hollow winds of the Autumn are here,
And the leaves of the forest are yellow and sear.

Now loiters the lazy mist sluggish and still,
On the side of the solitary songless hill,
The verdure has vanish'd, the beautiful green,
And the rich tints of Autumn embellish the scene.

Yes, Autumn has come, mellow, pensive and sad,
In her many-hued robe of loveliness clad,
And scarcely a breeze o'er the mountain's brow blows,
As th' wide-spreading woods in their calmness repose.

But Winter will come—'tis now heard in the breeze,
That th' fast-fading foliage strips from the trees,
And soon it shall mantle the earth with its shroud,
As age brings its white locks when manhood is bow'd.

THE FALL OF THE YEAR.

Fair Spring, the bland mother of bright months has
    past,
  All the glory of Summer 's gone by,
And the farewell of Autumn is heard in the blast,
  As it fitfully sweeps o'er the sky.

When I gaze on the sky, with its canopy high,
  Where the clouds by the tempests are driv'n,
Then I think of the day, when it shall pass away,
  By the time-rending trumpet's tone riv'n.

When I look at the forest, so verdant of late,
  With its branches now leafless and bare,
I'm admonish'd it is, too, mortality's fate,
  Which I sooner or later must share.

When I look at the leaves, as they lie on the ground,
  They tell me of death and decay,
And remind me that all things material are bound
  For to moulder again into clay.

So to being thus rises, and ripens, and dies,
  All that is lovely, beautiful, bright,
All that glads the green earth, or that glows in the
    skies,—
  All must bow to time's pitiless blight.

Thus man from his cradle, goes forth for the grave,
Nor recks it how fair, or virtuous, or brave;
The sunshine of life must be changed for its gloom,
The flowers of youth, mark the path to the tomb.

But Spring, with her sun-gleam shall visit again,
Yon bleak mountain brow, and yon desolate glen,
And 'mong the green branches the glad birds shall
        sing,
And wave on the soft air their swift joyous wing.

So man (the material) may rot 'neath the clod,
But again he shall rise,— shall rise like a God:
Shall come up from his deep, his dark dusty bed,
With eternity's sunshine bright o'er his head.

WINTER.

Now pile up the wood, and rouse the bright fire,
For winter is here, and reckless his ire:
The hoary old eld comes sternly at last,
His ice-car is yoked to the fierce north blast;
He comes from the realms of the cold polar star,
From the frost-bound land of his might afar,
The winds are his steeds, the snow-storm his path,
And th' elements all are the slaves of his wrath.
The pitiless monarch, now rides on the storm,

With icicled locks, and frost-fretted form,
With cold glassy eyes, and keen bitter breath,
He looks,—and there is the image of death;
He breathes, chilling life intensely around;
And nature is wither'd, and seal'd is the ground;
He fetters the river, and on the bold steep
He grasps the bright stream in its glittering leap;
Th' forest stands leafless, all 'reft and aghast,
And creaks its stiff limbs as th' despot rides past;
Few are its wand'rers, on foot or on wing,
No warbler th' tyrant a welcome will sing.
Each creature dismay'd, droops moody and still,
And voiceless the valley, and voiceless the hill;
E'en babbling echo in deep slumber seems,
Save when by th' rifle aroused from her dreams.
Vegetation all rests, imprisoned in earth,
Till warm vernal suns shall wake it to birth,
Till nature shall change her vestal of white,
That glistens and gleams in th' noontide of light,
For garments of green, and wreaths of fair flow'rs,
When Spring leadeth on the bright sunny hours,
And glads with her beauty, forest and field,
And to her bland smiles, th' stern tyrant shall yield.

THE SNOW.

Now soft and silent from above,
Like mercy from the Throne of Love,
Heaven casts on earth its vesture white,
The spotless image of its light.
See dimly waving through the sky
The downy flakes incessant fly,
Resting their feathery load on all,
The tender twig, the cedar tall,
The graceful poplar straight and slim,
The aged oak, the knarled limb,
The lowly vale, the silent copse,
The level mead, the mountain tops,—
Immantled all in silvery light they shine,
And own the hand that clothed them was divine.
But eve comes on, now clear and cold,
The silvery whiteness gleams with gold.
How great! how lovely! and how grand!
The works of thy Almighty hand;
The seasons as they roll, proclaim
Thy power and goodness are the same.
Nor budding Spring, nor Summer's ray,
Alone delight, and love display,
But Autumn too, as round her fruits she casts,
And Winter, with her storms and northern blasts.

ON THE LATE SPRING OF 1843.

RUDE WINTER! long has been thy reign,
Upon the mountain, and the plain;
Reluctant long, wert thou to yield,
Thy rule o'er forest, flower, and field;
Though Spring with tearful eye was seen,
And angel smile, and youthful mein,
To woo thee from thy stern intent,
That seem'd on nature's ruin bent;
Though coy and bashful, long she strove
Thy icy hand and heart to move,
And gently from thy grasp to gain
Her wonted right on earth to reign.
E'en beauty's power the hoar eld felt;
His frost-bound heart began to melt,
His iron hand relaxed at last,
The sceptre fell; and on the blast,
Mutt'ring to northern realms he past.
She claim'd it hers, and round her drew
Her robe of bright ethereal blue:
The flowers sprung up beneath her tread;
A crown of sunshine clothed her head;
A wreath of roses girt her vaist,
As up from earth she rose in haste.
O'er her domain a smile she threw,
And Winter's ling'ring shades withdrew;
She breathed—and balmy was the air,
Whispers of love, that checl'd despair,
Upon the floating breeze wee heard,

That through the leafless branches stirr'd,
While soft as falling tears, came showers,
Succeeded soon by sunny hours.
    Nature looked up with cheerful eye,
She saw the wintry storm was by,
She doffed her mourning — put on green,
While peeping buds, and flowers were seen,
With blushing charms, and odors sweet,
Expanding Spring's warm kiss to meet;
The humming bird, on tiny plume,
Was visiting the bursting bloom;
While sportive tribes of insects play,
Upon the life-awakening ray;
And blackbird, jay, and turtle-dove
On every tree told tales of love;
All that had voice, Spring's welcome sung;
And heaven and earth with rapture rung.
Let man the strain prolong, and raise
To God his gratitude and praise.

LINES TO J. P.

It's not in resentment thy love I resign;
I blame not, upbraid not, one motive of thine;
I ask not what change has come over thy heart;
I ask not what chance have doom'd us to part;
I but know by action—I must admire thee no more,
And still must obey where I once did adore.

HIS ANSWER.

IN sorrow I learn from thy beautiful line,
I've unconsciously wounded that bosom o' thine;
I err'd, it is true, but I err'd not in heart;
I ask should such chances then doom us to part?
If I've caused thee one tear, or wak'd one regret,
I know that thou still canst forgive and forget;
I know that I love thee, nay almost adore,
And for what thou hast written, I love thee the more.

A WINTER SCENE.

O YE! who with life's luxuries are blest,
And nightly on your downy pillows rest.
Who loll at ease in warm well-furnished rooms,
Where want nor winter scarcely ever comes;
Whose frames are clad by Fashion's costly hand;
Who feast upon the fattest of the land :
Around whose pathway wealth profusely flings
The varied blessings fickle fortune brings;
Who feel no inward dread, nor anxious fear,
While art defies the tyrant of the year.
Ye sons of soft indulgence! and ye fair!
Whose forms the flaunting robes of fashion bear;
Votaries of pride and folly! ye know not

One half the sorrows of the poor man's lot—
The ills, the hardships, struggles, cares and woes,
That rend *his* heart, and hinder *his* repose.

All day the wintry winds that wailed without,
With fury whirled the fleecy storm about,
And many a wreath of drifted snow was seen,
Ere came the ruddy sunset, cold and keen:
While from the west of the cerulean sky,
The young moon looked with half averted eye,
And all the stars that e'er graced heaven's arch,
Went forth that evening on their midnight march;
The biting frost intensely breathed around;
The floods were fettered, and seal'd fast the ground,
And naught was heard amid the whitened waste,
Save the wild murmurs of the passing blast;
I heard —'twas fancy—no, I heard a groan—
How full of misery that plaintive tone!
Of anguish, and despair, and mental strife,
Far fiercer than the pangs of parting life:
I listened till I found those accents flowed
From yonder hovel's comfortless abode;
I knew as on the fitful gust they swept,
Father and family together wept.
Once he was fortune's favorite — but oh!
In want and wretchedness she laid him low:
Frowned on his fate, and blasted it with gloom,
Though long he proudly struggled 'gainst his doom,
Till from each hope by disappointment driv'n,
His only hope was in the grave—and Heav'n.
Then ruthless, unrelenting Winter saw
Those trembling wretches on their couch of straw;

All destitute of fuel, food, and fire,
With scarce a ray to screen them from his ire,
While the congealing night-wind rudely rolled,
And to the ear this tale of sorrow told.
Alas! the picture's not o'erwrought, nor rare,
Thou wealthy, proud professor, then beware,
God holds thee guilty, if thou hast forgot,
The care He claimeth for the poor man's lot.

THE INDIAN.

O! let the white man ne'er forget,
The red man once his wigwam set,
Upon the site his footsteps tread,
Where scenes of commerce now are spread.

These hills he roam'd with arrow fleet,
Himself almost as swift of feet;
These hills were lit with th' lurid glance
Of council fire, 'mid th' mystic dance.

And where the moonlight's gentle gleam
Glides through the thicket on the stream,
The youthful Indian oft has hied,
And woo'd at eve his sunburnt bride.

All these were his, to him were given
By the all-wise bequest of Heaven,

Ere bold Columbus tracked the seas,
And braved the billow and the breeze..

But science, like some distant star,
Beam'd on his spirit from afar,—
With prescient hope, another world
He sought, and there his flag unfurl'd.

With (Art and Science in its train)
The wings of commerce cross'd the main,
All that was good, or great, or fair,
Found residence and shelter there.

Now o'er the broad scarce-bounded scene,
Are plenty, peace, and freedom seen;
God has designed in later days,
Truth's mighty temple here to raise.

But, ah! there is that still must mar,
The glory of thy brightest star—
It is a stain of crimson guilt,
It is the blood of Indians, spilt.

No more let history inscribe,
Oppression to the savage tribe;
Pity the injured Indian race,
Nor drive him from his resting place.

THE LYRE OF FREEDOM.

A FRAGMENT.

When Burns the startling summons gave,
And roused to victory or the grave,
Renowned Scotia's hardy son,
His plume, and plaid, and tartar on;
How quick the work of death was done.
To glory, too, the gallant Gaul,
Woke, at the poet's thrilling call,
Armed in his injured country's cause,
And bade the tyrant despot pause.
The poet's song, and raptured ryme,
In every age and every clime,
Had power—if not, as some relate,
To move e'en things inanimate—
To urge the high impetuous soul,
Or bid the gentle tear-drop roll.

   *   *   *   *

'T is not for him whose only aim
Is worldly gain, or worldly fame;
Far above these his soul must mount,
And drink from the celestial fount;
And sweep the bold extatic lyre,
That genius, truth, and love inspire.

CHANGE.

O Change! creation owns thy power,
   And bows to thy command;
Press'd to thy work, each swift-wing'd hour,
   With sure unerring hand,
Its impress true on all applies,
And finishing its labor, flies.
There's naught escapes thy searching sway,
Though hidden from the blaze of day;
Though mured in Egypt's arid cave,
That seemeth being's changeless grave;
Though buried deep on ocean's floor,
O'er which the welt'ring billows roar;
Though in the dark and silent earth,
The fruitful womb of being's birth,
Whence all her countless forms arise,
As matter buds, matures, and dies;
There's nought in ocean, earth, or sky,
But thou wilt seal its destiny.
  O Change! thy servitor, Decay,
    Is ever in the rear,
  To track thee on thy wond'rous way,
    And with dark death to sear
Whate'er material thou hast taught
To live, and bloom, with beauty fraught.
Man's mortal frame, with every breath,
Is hurrying on with haste to death.
Earth's loveliest flower ere eve may fade,

And withered on her lap be laid.
The giant oak, though strong and tall,
Thy might confesses in its fall;
All have their youth, climax, decay—
To death conducts the rip'ning ray;
With silent but progressive power,
Thou thus shalt rule each year and hour,
Until the fiery god of day,
Himself shall bow beneath thy sway.
   O Change! thy melancholy story,
     Is writ upon the past—
   Upon the wrecks of perished glory,
     That o'er the world are cast,
Like fragments rising from the deep,
Where dark oblivion's waters sweep.
The palace proud, with ivied crest,
The crumbling castle, battle's breast,
The abbey hoar, with cloister'd monk,
All works of art, to ruin sunk;
Palmyra's colonades and aisles,
Egypt's hieroglyphic piles,
Athenean beauty, Roman pride,
Pompeii rescued from time's tide—
All speak with eloquence, and tell
Of those who 'neath thy power have fell.
Thine is the tide, whose onward wave,
Has made this world a mighty grave;
While tears in torrents have been wept,
As one by one, thy fury swept,
From regal hall, or cottage hearth,
The mighty, or the loved of earth.

But Change ! there's mercy in thy might,
   There's beauty in thy power,
Good, in the darkness and the light,
   And love in every hour:
And storms, than sunny hours no less,
The goodness of a God express.

LIBERTY.

The voice of Liberty is heard,
   Echoing from every land;
'Mutual rights,' is her watch-word,
   And Truth alone her brand.

Green Erin's harp, its stirring strain,
   To liberty has woke ;
And sea-girt Albion's sons disclaim
   Th' oppressor's servile yoke.

The Russian despot's frigid sky,
   Once heard its thrilling tone;
The noble Poles expiring cry,
   Its energy has shown.

The high-born Greek by freedom bade,
   Threw back the tyrant's claim,
And brandish'd his avenging blade,
   For liberty and fame.

Nor long shall superstition hold,
  In bonds th' immortal mind :
Virtue and truth have made man bold,
  Its shackles to unbind.

The sceptre, powerless, from the grasp
  Of tyrant hands must fall :
And Worth alone, that sceptre clasp,
  If clasp'd again at all.

Sweet mountain Nymph ! pure Nature's child !
  O Liberty, art thou !
Loving the forest's lonely wild,
  The rugged steep, and barren brow.

From courtly pride thou erst hast fled,
  And sought this woody shore,
Whose sons for thee have nobly bled,
  Whose sons thy name adore.

AMERICA.

Where's Babylon, the first empire?
  Where now her ramparts rise ?
And where is lofty Babel's pyre,
  Peering in eastern skies?

E

And where Assyria, famed of old?
   That great but wicked nation;
Along whose streets the prophet told,
   Its dread denunciation.

And Egypt where? where first the light
   Of science gleam'd obscure?
And as in dark oblivion's spite,
   Rear'd the stupendous tower.

Greece! where is thy arcadian bower,
   Where Art and Science dwelt?
Where is the sumptuous Persian power,
   And he Heav'n's vengeance dealt?

And Alexander, who unfurl'd
   Boundless power's pennon, now?
While the laurels of a conquer'd world,
   Wreath'd his ambitious brow.

O Rome! and tarnish'd is thy glory!
   Has genius fled the scene?
Still sculptured fragments tell the story,
   Of much that thou hast been.

The weed has round thy relics clung,
   And ages o'er thee swept,
And Time her awful requiem sung,
   And many a spirit wept.

America! to thee, blest land,
   I turn, from empire's fall,

O'er whom stern fate's imperious hand
  Has spread oblivion's pall.

To thee, who phœnix-like art merging,
  From many a nation's wreck:
Like to the morning sun's bright verging,
  Or beams that night bedeck.

Behold it stretch'd from sea to sea,
  From day-spring to its goal,
And like its wand'ring rivers, free,
  Like its oceans, no control.

Her ample lap with blessings teeming,
  And beauty o'er her soil,
And her high mountain peaks are gleamig,
  With Heaven's propitious smile.

A voice is on her mighty waters,
  A voice is on her floods,
Heard, joyous by her sons and daughters,
  In her primeval woods.

It is the voice of Liberty,
  That on her rivers roll'd,
As on deep murm'ring to the sea,
  The sacred theme they told.

The dwellers on the rock and mountain,
  Have bid its chorus rise:
Forth-bursting like the bright pure fountain,
  That from their bosom hies.

It has reach'd th' forest's sunless glen,
 And mingled with the blast,
That rose and told the joy, and then
 In deeper accents past.

Nor Liberty alone is thine:
 'T were madness uncontrolled:
But science, art, and truth divine,
 Thy sacred laws uphold.

Where hatred-burning savage bands
 Raised the red scalping knife,
And tomahawk, with cruel hands,
 Rush'd to the bitter strife:

Where was the Indian war-whoop heard,
 The frenzied wild poo-whoo,
Is preach'd the everlasting word,
 The truth in Jesus now.

For sybil songs, and demon spells,
 Mutter'd in mystic tone,
Whose meaning there one stands and tells,
 Amidst the throng alone—

Reason, her dignity displays,
 And Genius rears her throne,
And with an eagle glance surveys
 A realm from zone to zone.

THE AMERICAN FLAG.

Where Licking's waters gently glide,
Deep murmuring to Ohio's tide;
And Arts with Nature's charms unite
The gazer's vision to delight:
There, on Kentucky's rugged shore,
That looks the lovely landscape o'er,
The flaunting banner of the brave
Floats gaily 'bove the glassy wave,
As in the sunset's golden light,
It flings its folds of crimson bright.
Ye stars and stripes! though now ye play
So peaceful in the evening ray,
Far other thoughts are waked by thee,
Proud banner of the brave and free!
Flaming along the path of war,
Thou wert of old the freeman's star,
On which he fixed his faithful eye,
And rushed to death or victory.
Thou wert to him a spirit form,
That hov'ring hung o'er battle's storm,
That fiercely gleamed through fire and smoke,
And vengeance in his bosom woke:
When trumpet called, when roll'd the drum,
That bade the bold to battle come—
When cannons roar'd, and bayonets glanced,
And foe to foe with haste advanced—
When rank and file in conflict clash'd,
As to the deadly strife they dash'd,

And the patriot fell in his red path,
The victim of the foeman's wrath;
On thee he'd lift his languid eye,
And 'neath thy folds exulting die.
When first was heard young Freedom's call,
That bade him burst oppression's thrall,
Thine was the spirit-stirring power,
That nerved him in the trying hour;
Thine was the potent heaven-born spell,
To which the might of tyrant's fell,
When victory perch'd upon thy crest,
And Liberty came there to rest.
In triumph thus forever wave,
Above the freeman's home and grave;
In beauty thus forever sweep,
On mountain top, on ocean's deep;
In glory thus forever shine,
Emblem of Freedom! and her shrine.

ENGLAND.

Thou gem of ocean! father-land!
Around thy bold and rocky strand
The white waves dash, and fret, and foam—
Can I forget thee, native home!

Roll on, ye waves! roll wild and free,
Around the island of the sea;

Your curling crests bear men as brave,
As ever met a briny grave.

Balmy and fresh thy ocean air,
Thy fields are fertile, flowery, fair;
Lovely and brave thy Saxon blood;
As thou art great, would thou wert good.

Ere Science on thee shed its ray,
Rome's eagle mark'd thee for her prey;
Thy chief, though chain'd, yet unsubdued,
The pomp of Rome undaunted view'd.

Alfred was thine, the peasant king,
Whom patriots laud, and poets sing;
Who infant freedom left his age,
And pour'd its light on history's page.

And Spencer, whose poetic fire
To rapture tuned the English lyre;
And Milton, whose seraphic muse
Time and eternity reviews.

And Shakspeare, of immortal fame,—
Deathless as nature is his name;—
Accomplish'd Pope, reflective Young,
And Cowper with his winning song.

Thine gifted Byron, much-loved White,
Pollok, who wing'd through time his flight;
These are thy sons, and these are names,
Mankind with thee in common claims :

And these are names that honor earth—
To man, to mind, of greater worth,
Than ought the belted warrior gains
From cities sack'd, or battle plains.

Thine philosophic Bacon too,
Who search'd material nature through;
And Newton, who with wing of light
Track'd the swift comet's wand'ring flight.

When superstition, like a cloud,
Cover'd the earth, and mind was how'd
Beneath the heavy Papal yoke,
Thy Wickliffe rose, and truth awoke.

From the dark cloud bright Genius burst,
Science and truth by thee were nurst,
Till the wild wave that wash'd thy shore,
Thy fame to every nation bore.

Till white-wing'd coursers of the sea,
From every climate rode to thee:
And proudly waved thy banner high,
In every port beneath the sky.

Till on thy wide extended sway,
Unceasing smiled the God of day;
And Neptune, monarch of the sea!
His ancient trident gave to thee.

" I love thee still"—but hate the sin
That works its baleful ill within,

That blights thy glory, blasts thy fame,
And makes thy offspring blush for shame:

That to a few gives place and power,
Makes penury the peasant's dower;
Scorns him who for his country bled—
Denies to toil the meed of bread.

May Albion hear,—hear truth's appeal;
Ere brandish'd is the rebel steel;
Within her own green vales may hide,
The spirit that shall curb her pride.

Albion! proud Island of the sea!
How many brave hearts beat in thee;
But those brave hearts may braver be,
When warm'd with love of Liberty.

IRELAND.

THERE is an Isle on Ocean's breast,
Round which the raging billows leap,
That rears aloft its emerald crest,
And smiles upon the ambient deep.

That Island is the loveliest gem,
On ocean's broad blue bosom seen,
There nature weaves her diadem
Of her loved shamrock's living green.

But what are nature's smiles to thee,
On ocean, hill, or verdant vale?
Son of the green Isle of the sea!
Say, what do all her charms avail?

So long as by oppression bound,
Thou sittest in the sordid dust,
And thy warm tears bedew the ground,
Clothing thy servile chains with rust.

Wake! Erin! wake thine harp once more,
Though riven now, and all unstrung—
That harp that through thy halls of yore,
With youthful freedom's music rung

That harp, whose deeply plaintive tone,
With every ruth and wrong was filled,
As by the wand'ring breezes blown,
Upon the patriot heart's it thrilled.

But list! the plain is past, the idle sigh
No more floats on the ocean's breath,
A loftier note, a nobler cry
Is heard, 'tis liberty or death.

Erin has risen in her might,
Her brave hand grasps the brandish'd steel,
And in her eye is freedom's light,
And on her tongue the cry, Repeal.

Onward! may heaven speed thee now,
The soul-degrading chain to sever,
If Truth and Freedom bid the blow,
Strike! they may be thine for ever.

INFIDELITY,

A TALE OF THE REVOLUTION.

HENRY MACFLENE, the hero of this history, was born in one of the eastern States, in the year 1758. His father, while young, had emigrated from Scotland; and being possessed of a small fortune, embarked in business, and by industry and economy acquired considerable wealth. In his character, kindness and generosity were mingled with the frugality of the Scotch, and consequently, while cautiousness marked all his undertakings, he was regarded as a man of enlightened liberality, and of public spirit. In 1756, he married a Canadian lady, of French extraction; one daughter, and the subject of this sketch, were the fruits of their union.

Mr. Macflene had naturally a strong constitution, and a vigorous meditative mind: there was a sedateness upon his brow, and a gravity of thought over his countenance, yet he had a soul alive to the keenest sensibilities of our nature. Happy in his partner, and their pleasing offspring, the cup of his domestic felicity seemed full. Home was the circle where he loved to move, and his fireside was the scene of order, instruction, and love.

Mrs. Macflene was a woman far more retired and domestic in her habits, than is usual in females of her descent; she was lovely in her person, and of the kindest disposition, and her affection for her husband and children appeared unbounded; but the ardent intellect and the intense solicitude of the father had induced him to supercede her in promoting the education of their children: their improvement and happiness seemed to be the end of his existence, and the centre of his earthly hopes: often might his firm-set eye have been seen to relax with delight, or to glitter with a tear, as he gazed upon their guileless gambols; he would even become a partner in their sports, and spend his intervals of leisure in the construction of their play-things. As they grew up, their moral and intellectual advancement gave a tone and direction to his conversation: books of simple illustration were put into their hands, and the beauties of nature pointed out to their admiring view. He would wander with them upon the sun-lit hill, when Spring was spreading abroad her green carpet, and gemming with bud and blossom the long desolate branch, while Nature's choristers were welcoming with new notes of joy her reviving beam, that was glittering in the glassy lake, or laughing in the rapid rill. The lovely, and the terrible; the whispering breeze, and the bursting thunder; the wood-crowned height, and the flower-gemmed vale; the glorious sky, and the changeful earth; all furnished ample sources for reflection and remark, calculated " to rear the tender thought," and lead the mind "from Nature, up to nature's God."

So rolled away the sunny days of youth, until Henry was thirteen, and his sister eleven years old, when they were sent by their reluctant parents to a select boarding school.

Delia, the daughter, was a fascinating little creature, with dark glossy curls that hung in rich profusion around her snowy neck; her features were remarkably expressive, and her eye shone with unwonted vivacity; but her form was feeble, and her health delicate; while her mind was sympathetic and susceptible in the extreme. Henry, too, was a lovely youth, with a countenance frank and unshaded; possessing a mind ardent and inquisitive, he early manifested a disposition for the pursuits of learning.

The admonitions of the parents had made an evident impression upon the minds of their children. They had early been taught to remember their Creator. They had been told of His love, who died that all might live; and as morning and evening came, had they bowed in lisping prayer at a mother's knee; consequently, their dispositions were such as to delight their doting parents, and to make them favorites abroad.

Their school was situated amidst the richly diversified and highly romantic scenery that adorns the banks of the Connecticut river, where three years glided away, fraught with all the unsuspecting joyfulness of youth. About this time Delia's health

began to decline. She had grown fast, and like the
premature blossoms of Spring, was about to wither;
her constitution was sensibly failing, she therefore
bade farewell to her much-loved governess and com-
panions, and, casting a "long, last, lingering look"
on scenes endeared by the fond recollections of child-
hood, returned to the parental roof.

Henry left not her side, but with a look of the
tenderest regard did he watch her wan and delicate
features: an insiduous disease was too visibly wind-
ing itself about her vitals, ere long to crush its
victim in its fatal folds. She lingered long; but as
life's fountain ebbed, her spirit seemed to brighten.
To her friends she was linked by the love of a pure
and grateful heart, which nothing but death could
sunder. She had gazed upon nature's loveliness,
and memory now cheered her chamber with the re-
collection of the happy hours when she gamboled
on the grassy sward, or frolic'd in the flowery vale,
and in the fulness of her joy twined in her glossy
curls the fragrant images of her own fair but frail
beauty. She repined not. Resignation rested upon
her beautiful features, which often even brightened
into mirth. She had not yet known the bitterness
of life's cup; her brow was unclouded by care, and
her eye unshadowed by suspicion; her cheek was
unblanched by guilty fear, and the freshness of her
lip untainted by the breath of unhallowed passion.
She had played about the fountain of life, and drank
of its unpolluted rills: she had plucked its sweetest
flowers, and rejoiced in the morning of her exist-
ence; while, as she looked along its opening vista,

Now broke the morning of the Revolution. Liberty! Liberty! was resounded through the land— re-echoed from the hill-top, and re-verbrated from the vale. The call of the hollow drum was heard, and the trumpet's brazen voice. The husband exchanged the prattle of his children, and the embraces of his wife, for the din of battle-strife, and to clasp, perchance in death, the blood-stained earth. The lover tore himself from the new-pledged maid; and brothers left the parental roof, loaded with kisses, caresses, and blessings on their cause. The son of the forest threw over his shoulder the murderous rifle, and congregated with the man of profession, the merchant, and the mechanic. Then the starried banner fluttered in the breeze; then was heard the martial music, and the heavy tramp; the roaring of artillery, and the clash of arms, with the flash, the smoke, and the shout of battle. The fire of freedom was in each breast, and young and old abandoned their firesides to defend their homes, and to assert their rights. Among them was Henry and his father; the latter fell at Bunker's Hill; his body was found covered with the slain, and his last words were said to be, ' God save my country !'

Henry continued some time in the service, and joined a detachment under Marquis Lafayette. He was promoted as Colonel, and distinguished himself by his bravery, intelligence and pleasing demeanor. He associated much with his fellow officers, many of whom were French. He mingled in their amusements, and was counted as the companion of their jolliest hours, for the sweetness of his manners, and

the playfulness of his repartee; though he partook
but sparingly of their excesses; while he caught
their manners, he unfortunately imbibed their infidel
principles, though not till after repeated sallies of
wit, argument, and ridicule, did he surrender.

There are minds that, once having formed an opin-
ion, tenaciously retain it, and, either from an inac-
tivity of intellect, or a selfish love of sentiment
which they have identified with themselves, ward
off every attempt to shake the fortress of their belief,
or disturb their indolent tranquility. There are oth-
ers, noble and ingenuous, whose minds are accessible
to truth, who throw off the fetters of early prejudice,
who disdain the trammels of sectarianism, and un-
folding before themselves the pages of knowledge,
seek to form their views on the broad basis of uni-
versal Truth; but who, alas! by their love of free
inquiry, are often led into the mazes of error and of
doubt. Such was young Macflene. He had seen
the happifying influence of religion on the feelings
and character of his parents, and from a filial fond-
ness had, in a great measure, drank into their views,
and participated of their principles. But these, his
first ideas, were the product of parental influence,
and not formed from personal observation, investiga-
tion, and reflection; therefore, when he went forth
into the world, and beheld the varying phases of so-
ciety, its infinity of sentiment, and the opposites of-
ten espoused by minds of the first order, of acknow-
ledged integrity, and of intellectual worth—when
he viewed infidelity, veiled with all the attractions
of youth, politenss, and education; it was no wonder

that the feeble fabric, thus unfort'fied, fell, and that his youthful impressions melted like the snow-wreath in the sunbeams. But though in ruins, th> relics of that fabric were there; and though those feelings, like the snow-wreath, had vanished, they had softened and enriched the soil, and still their influence was felt.

He now stumbled at the mysteries of Revelation, and was unwilling to believe that which he could not comprehend. He sought to understand that which the mind of man was never formed to grasp. He vainly grappled with Infinity, and attempted, on reason's pinions, to scale the Throne of God, and with its scanty plummet, to sound the deeps of Revelation and of Providence. But ah! its depths mocked the reach of reason, and her waxen wings melted beneath the brightness of the Eternal: bedizzed and confounded, he fell, and reason seemed to reel. For awhile the hour of conviviality lost to him its relish and delight; and though he occasionally mingled in the festive scene, and parried the passing joke, conscience still lingered at his heart, and pictured upon the walls of his festivity the hand that wrote his doom. 'That dread of something after death,' still haunted his imagination, which he would still strive to allay, as the phantom of fanaticism and of early education. . He revolted against his Maker. He had put his foot from off the haven-bound vessel of Eternal Truth, and in his own little bark, had ventured forth upon the broad and hoisterous ocean of uncertainty. His polar star, obscured by the clouds of skepticism—yea, hidden in the night of Infidelity. His charter of Eternal Truth thus discarded, he was now a creature of chance, and his bright intellectual faculties believed to cease with his mortal existence.

His companions saw their triumph, and left nothing wanting to complete it. Closer, though almost imperceptibly, they drew around him the meshes of his captivity, and by their fascinations beguiled him farther and farther into the vortex of dissipation.

As a soldier, many were the changes and chances to which he was exposed; but we shall not here attempt to follow him to the encampment, the parade, and the scene of action. The detachment had been stationed for a short time in the village of Fairfax, and were preparing to march to meet Gen. Washington, when Henry received a letter from his mother, informing him she was sick, and anxiously pressing his return home. She was now a widow, and some affairs belonging to her late husband remained unsettled. He was, however, reluctant to comply; the wreath of victory invited him forward, and the laurels of his country's independence were yet ungathered; he therefore referred the matter to the Marquis, who, while he applauded his patriotic devotion to their cause, and regretted the loss they would sustain, generously advised his return. With heartfelt sorrow he exchanged the firm grasp with his gallant comrades, and saw, with mingled feelings of regret and admiration, the bright cavalcade move glittering along, with their noble commander in the front, and the rustic though no less effective provincials in their rear, who were seen sallying forth with the spirits of freemen, and with sinewy forms, from their native villages, the fields that their childhood knew, and their own bright hearths, to meet the foe. There, then, were the matron's last words of advice, the last looks of bright-eyed girls; children with lisping lips and sunny faces, hanging round the athletic limbs of their fathers; old men, with tottering limb and broken voice, encouraging their sons to deeds of daring, while the glow of freedom quickened their lagging blood, and lit afresh their time-worn features. But they are gone: and the gazing crowd slowly retires; while here and there are seen knots of grey-headed politicians, groups of pensive and musing maidens, and of prayerful and anxious wives and mothers.

Not unknown, nor unobserved, was the young Colonel, as he passed among them. His manly bearing and fine form, set off by military costume, must have caught their attention, had he not been already known and admired.

The detachment having been quartered for some time in the village, Henry had contracted an acquaintance with some of its honest and open-hearted inhabitants, that perhaps amounted to something more than friendship; and various were the greetings which he met, as he walked down to his quarters.

There was a neat-looking white frame on the roadside, with green window blinds, and a pretty romantic porch, over which rambled the vagrant tendrils of a vine, mingling with roses that hung around in rich profusion. Henry had become acquainted with its inmates, and was accustomed, not unfrequently, to

call and taste the unsophisticated sweets of rural so-
ciety. The old people, though English by birth,
were staunch republicans in principle. With his
four sons, Mr. Barton—for such was his name—was
gone to contend for his country. At the garden gate
still stood the mother and her two daughters, a
neighbor's girl, and an old uneducated domestic who
had emigrated with the family to this country. As
he approached, a smile arose on each countenance,
while the fair cheek of *one* might have been observed
to receive an additional tinge.

Good morning Colonel! said the mother.

Good morning, Madam! Good morning, ladies!
was the reply.

I hear, Colonel, that you remain. How is that?
for I am sure they need such as you.

Yes, madam, fate has this time compelled me to
turn my back on my enemies, and robbed me of the
conqueror's wreath. I must return to console a sick
and a widowed mother.

Ah, well-o-day! a pity o' that; but, as they say,
' the braver the man the warmer the heart.' May
God bless them and their noble Commander.

Yes, madam, my heart is with them.

Young gentleman — muttered old Robin, the do-
mestic — I think your heart is nearer hum. I guess
youn a ankerin after some gal, or you'd be wi' um
yoursel.

Robin, you speak before your turn. Though,
Colonel, there may be something in it?—said the old
lady.

Madam!—said he, casting a furtive glance at the

lovely listeners—if such was my aim, I might well · wish to remain here.

Miss Ellen, to whom his eye had been more particularly directed, blushed and smilled, as, with her companions, she curtesied to the compliment.

You have lovely flowers,—said he archly, plucking three roses and politely handing them to the girls, whose whispers and inuendoes soon indicated that Ellen had received the finest.

But they are not without their thorns—replied the mother, whose keen eye quickly noticed his pleasautry, and its effects.

They are sweet, if they have thorns—returned the Colonel, as he gathered one for himself, bowed, and retired, amidst the smiles and invitations of the agreeable group.

Henry, now arranged for his departure, paid his last visit to his country friends, not forgetting Mrs. Barton and her fair Ellen. But filial affection urged him away. He departed —determined to pursue the study of his profession, and to devote himself to the comfort and the happiness of his remaining parent. He arrived. How all was changed! The companions of his youth were dispersed: the scenes of his boyhood had vanished: the 'march of intellect' had been there; and improvements had arisen rapidly around. He found his mother but a relic of what she once was: sorrow had wasted her; and the ravages of age and sickness were upon her; but his presence cheered and revived her; and under his affectionate attentions her health was partially restored.

The mother's soul was now bound up in her son: he was her all. With what doting delight would her eye wander over his manly form, improved and matured as it was by years, and his face beaming with all the expressions of intellect and honor; little dreaming, as yet, that the seeds of religious principle which she had assisted in planting, had but put forth and blossomed, to be blasted by infidelity, and almost forgotten amid the blandishments of society. Though not entirely confirmed in his infidel principles, conscience was stifled, and he seemed to have sunk into a state of apathy and indifference; but her conversation aroused him, and ere long she discovered the drift of his mind, and the vast change which his feelings had undergone. Often would she reason with him, and endeavor to reclaim him; but his superior intellect and information baffled every attempt, and ultimately she surrendered her own views to the sympathy of maternal affection, and to the power of his eloquence. He gathered around them all the charms of genteel life, and strove to promote her comfort and her happiness. He successfully prosecuted his profession, living chiefly in town, though his mother resided in a house built by his father, but a few miles distant, where he often repaired for study or for relaxation; and sought relief in its calmness and seclusion, when jaded with the jostling world, or with the conflicts of his own spirit; for, though the surface seemed smooth, beneath the violence of the tempest was yet unstilled.

The midnight hour was past, and the expiring lamp threw its faint glimmer upon the ranged bookshelves and on the thought-paled features of the student, admonishing him that its oil was nearly spent. Absorbed in thought, he threw himself back in his chair: before him lay the Holy Scriptures and various infidel productions, indicating that the theme of his research and intense investigation had been, the existence of a Deity—the origin, nature and relations of man. A painful expression passed over his features as he rose from his seat and walked forth upon the balcony. The moon, in her effulgence, was walking amid the bright watchers of heaven, and smiling upon her sister earth, now reposing in loveliness and peace; while the scarcely stirring zephyr swept, with its light pinion, his feverish brow. All was still, save his own soft foot-fall, and the ceaseless murmur of the distant stream. He stood and looked upon the lovely scene, that by its beauty seemed to invite him to the contemplation of nature, and of nature's God. His mind strove to unfetter itself from the theories and sophistries with which it was entangled: and while, as with the wonder of a first sight, he viewed with admiration the far-lit prospect, its etherial calmness soothed his soul into tranquility; and as he gazed upon the mysterious beauty of the luminaries of heaven, and thought upon their order, the regularity of their movements uninterrupted by terrestrial influences, imagination soared beyond peopling immensity with mind. For a moment the whispers of infidelity were hushed, the vagaries of chance, and the hypothesis of an eternal succession, vanished; and Reason essayed to rest upon the credence of an Allwise, Almighty, Creating

Power. The fire of devotion was kindling upon the altar of his heart, and his proud spirit bowed with reverence and awe. But the clouds gathered fast over that starried canopy, and the glittering scene was soon clothed with obscurity and darkness. He retired to his chamber, confused and dejected. Life, too, thought he, is but a continual struggle betwixt light and shade. How few, and how short, its intervals of peace! How many are the bright visions that hope has called forth, thus quickly to be blasted! And Truth! 'tis dim and uncertain as the moonlight landscape. Oh! could I credit the christian's creed, how would I covet his unflattering faith. Then might I look to Him as my polar star; and through the gloom of Time look forward to an eternal day; then, with the poet, might I pity those

"Whose hope still lingers in this dark sojourn,
While lofty souls who look beyond the tomb,
Can smile at fate, and wonder why they mourn."

But ah! it cannot be. The clouds of skepticism are over me, and the labyrinth of infidelity is around me. Wearied and exhausted with application, he threw himself upon his bed, and sunk into a restless slumber.

The sun had made some hours travel up its blue broad pathway, ere he awoke in moody and musing frame. His mind still vacillated; but he seemed determined to defend the system he had unfortunately espoused. His mother, kind and passive, coincided in all things with the idol of her heart, and was anxious to encourage him in the prospects of future eminence, which she believed his talents were opening up before him.   But ere long she sickened; and he endeavored to sustain and sooth her by his false philosophy; but a fatal fever was at her vitals, that, like a fury, drank at the fountain of her life, and revelled amid the ruins it so rapidly had wrought. Her lucid intervals were few; while words of thrilling import, shrieks, and agonizing gestures, told the anguish of her soul; and thus she died.   Her last moments were rational, but unhappy; and her last words were, Henry! Henry! Henry!—He stood as transfixed, gazing on that dying hour; his eye quailed not, but the violence of mental agony quivered upon his lips, and his nerves occasionally shook with a quick involuntary shudder.   He saw the light fade from her glazing eye; he beheld the last convulsive throb of departing life; and the stupor of insensibility came over him; nor waked he from that dream, until the grave had received the remains of her he held dearest upon earth.

Now was his proud spirit humbled and subdued, and he fell in deep contrition before Him he had dared to contemn.   Now he saw the weakness of reason, the fallacy of Infidelity, and its fearful impotency in the hour of death; and while the expiring accents of his mother rung in his ear, and wrought his soul to wretchedness, in true penitence and prayer he bowed before his God, and found forgiveness.   He believed, embraced, and realized the blessings of Christianity.

He remembered Ellen Barton, sought and married her, and lived a long and useful life.

[NOTE.—Some of the foregoing pieces were written in more youthful days, and but few of them with a design to publication—such portions of the work are more adapted to youth, but it is hoped they will not be uninteresting to the general reader.]

ERRATA.—On page 36, for Sapphire, read SAMPHIRE.

In the 12th line of the same article, for had gave, read, STILL gave.

INDEX.

CPSIA information can be obtained
at www.ICGtesting.com
Printed in the USA
BVHW04*1705180918
527708BV00030B/1866/P